THE HARD COPY

THE HARD COPY

Candice Dela Cruz

Katherine Kurowski

Gihad Nasr

Maria Rivera

Life Rattle Press  Toronto, Canada

The Hard Copy

Published by Life Rattle Press, Toronto, Canada

Copyright 2016 by the contributing authors:

Candice Dela Cruz
Katherine Kurowski
Gihad Nasr
Maria Rivera

All rights reserved. The use of any part of this publication reproduced, transmitted in any form or by any means, electronic, mechanical, photocopying, recording or otherwise, or stored in a retrieval system, without the prior consent of the author is an infringement on the copyright law.

(New writers series ISSN 1200-5266)

ISBN 978-1-987936-28-5 (pbk.)

Acknowledgements:
The definition of "Loss" on page 1 in this publication comes from the
Paperback Oxford Canadian Dictionary
Katherine Barber edition,
Oxford University Press, New York, 2004.

Contents

Editing Tips 2

Chapter One
Burgundy Wayfarer 7
Context 11
First Impressions 15

Chapter Two
Beksa Lala 19
Economy 24
Stylistic Editing 27

Chapter Three
Missed Call 31
Parallelism 34
Copyediting 36

Chapter Four
Only a Shell 41
Active Voice 46
Compiling the Manuscript 49

loss *n*. **1 a** the act or an instance of losing; the state of being lost. **b** the fact of being deprived of a person by death, estrangement, etc. **2** a person, thing, or amount lost. **3** the detriment or disadvantage resulting from losing. **at a loss (sold etc.)** for less than was paid for it. **be at a loss** be puzzled or uncertain. **be at a loss for words** not know what to say.

Editing Tips

- **Do not edit your own story.** You can't always see your errors or whether you omitted contextual information.

- **Read the whole story first.** Understand the story's context before suggesting edits.

- **Query the author.** Do not hesitate to ask the author when in doubt of a fact, a name's spelling, a story's meaning, or a stylistic preference. After all, it's the author's story.

- **Use your dictionary, thesaurus, and style manual.** Check unfamiliar words. For example, verify whether a compound word is open, solid or hyphenated, or whether the word's first letter is capitalized or not.

- **Keep a style sheet handy.** Record all stylistic preferences. Consistency is important to maintain.

- **Provide constructive criticisms.** Explain the rationale behind suggested edits. When providing feedback, always make sure that the criticism is fair.

- **Cut appropriately.** While considering the context, cut unnecessary words, details, paragraphs, and even sections that do not support the story. Extraneous details are unnecessary and wordy sentences disrupt flow. Keep the story tight.

- **Take breaks.** Spending too much time revising can cloud the mind, cause you to overlook errors, and leave you mentally drained.

- **Remember the author.** The story belongs to the author. There are some stylistic preferences that, although grammatically correct, you may not personally like, but the author does. Leave the choice to the author.

Chapter One

loss *n.* a person or object that one looks for but never finds.

Burgundy Wayfarer

Candice Dela Cruz

I dip my toes into the grey sand and glare at the grey sky and hear the grey waves leap on the shore. The sand crushes against my feet as I walk. Ate—older sister in Filipino—crouches beside the sea.

"Mom said to find Dad," I say.

"Dad? I haven't seen him." Ate pokes a jellyfish with a twig.

Screeching sirens pierce the air. Ate's eyes widen. Women in bikinis and men in neon shorts swim back to land.

"Attention! Please avoid the sea until the typhoon Ondoy has passed. Again, avoid the sea until the typhoon Ondoy has passed," the lifeguard warns with his megaphone.

"Let's hurry." I clench Ate's drenched shirt.

She pats my head. "It's not yet raining. There's still time." She points in the distance. "Everyone is running to that crowd. Dad might be there." She yanks me up and runs into the water.

"Wait! The sea is dangerous." I pull her arm but she shakes it off. Going deeper, she wobbles from the waves.

"Shhh. Swimming's faster than walking on sand. Come here." She taps the dark tide.

I sneak into the sea while the lifeguards walk away. Approaching the abyss, I feel the water rise to my waist. Ate shoves me under water. I slap her hand and gasp for air.

"What are y—"

A gigantic wave slams my face and salt water fills my mouth. I extend my neck to face the sky and breathe.

"You're so slow," Ate says as I hold on to her tall frame. "C'mon! Let's dive."

I take a deep breath and sink. The kelp scratches my skin and the bubbles fizz as we paddle. Subtle noises echo underwater, so we swim upwards.

Ate surfaces first and lifts me up. Her face pales, her palms cover her mouth, and her gaze fixates on a white cloth that covers lifeless limbs. The corpses stack with their bodies bent in strange positions. A lifeguard resuscitates a girl wearing her Disney Princess swimsuit. My stomach tightens.

We wade towards the crowd until the water drops to my knees. I want to ask Ate whether Dad is in the pile. Instead I bite my chapped, salty lips. A sharp whistle pierces my ears.

"Get out of there," a lifeguard shouts. The whistling continues until we reach the shore. I head to our cottage, but Ate grabs me by my hair.

"Stop. Before we go, let's check what's happening." Her bloodshot eyes stare at me.

I tiptoe behind the crowd hovering over the bodies. I want a better view of the pile, but I only see wrinkled, pale toes.

"What's that?" Ate stares at a blue tarpaulin with a silver Rolex, coin purses, pocketbooks, rosaries, necklaces, gold bangles, Havaianas flip-flops, and Ray-Bans.

We shove through the crowd until we reach the tarpaulin.

Ate's palm wraps my wrist. "Kill me if we find Dad's stuff," she titters.

My eyes trace the rows of jewellery, belts, cell phones, and eyeglasses.

Ate's grip tightens. She eyes a pair of burgundy wayfarer eyeglasses – the same as Dad's. Her eyebrows knit together.

"Can we take this?" Ate asks the old lady manning the tarpaulin.

The old lady shrugs, "It doesn't matter. Whoever owns it might be dead."

Ate pinches my cheek. "Are you crying?" She asks.

My sight blurs. "What if Dad died?" I rub my eye and smear sand on my face.

"Don't jinx it." Ate wipes my forehead. A dimple dips beside her lips. "Don't lose hope." As we leave the crowd, she tosses her arm around me.

We climb the bamboo stairs that lead to our cottage. We knock on the cottage's rattan door and it swings open. Mom embraces us.

"I watched the local news. Are you okay?" Mom panics. She checks our legs and arms, and feels our foreheads. "I'm glad you're safe. Where's Dad?"

Ate hands her the glasses.

"Where did you get this?" Mom gasps. A vein bulges on her temple.

"The beach. There were bodies and a blue sheet with lost things," Ate says

Mom collapses onto a chair and buries her face in her arms atop the glass table. "No, no, no. Please," she cries, her words muffled. Her knuckles hit the table. "Ay! Noel!"

"He's not dead. It's probably not Dad's," Ate says calmly.

Mom dials Dad's number on her flip phone. The phone rings, but the sound fades. Mom drinks a water bottle until it's empty.

"We'll be fine," Mom reassures us. "He's not dead until I see his body," Mom declares and forces a smile. Ate nods and links arms with me.

Mom cranks up the volume on the TV. We huddle on the sofa and watch the news. I look at the crooked wall clock. Mom checks her phone again. Ate naps on my shoulder. My eyes dart from Mom's phone to the clock, to the dusty TV screen, and to the windowpanes dripping with rain. Red and blue lights flash through the windows, startling me.

"Mama, look!" I tug Mom's dress. The door shakes under heavy knocks. Mom rushes across the mahogany planks to pull the curtains aside. She peers outside. Mom twists the doorknob, grips on the diamond necklace that Dad gave her, and eases the door open.

A man stands with his arms wrapped around himself. A puddle pools around his bare feet.

"Noel!" Mom strikes Dad's chest. His thin build cradles Mom.

"I'm home," Dad says.

"Where were you?" Mom yells, tugging him into the house. She gives Dad a towel. "What happened?"

"I swam but my glasses fell into the water. I looked for them, then my leg cramped. I wanted to go home but I couldn't see or walk well. Luckily, the police gave me a ride," Dad grins.

"Are these yours?" Mom pulls the burgundy wayfarers from her pocket.

Dad squints at the glasses and puts them on. He looks around the living room. "They're not clear," he says.

Ate removes the glasses from Dad. "We'll just buy a new pair," she says.

Context

Context sets the story's circumstance by giving meaning to actions and feelings, hinting the setting's location and time, and clarifying the story's purpose and theme. An editor must detect when a story loses context. The reader should not be confused, lost, or bored because the story does not make sense.

Careless cutting of words can weaken a writer's ability to convince readers. Our editing group faced this challenge when we reduced our story from two thousand to one thousand words. When a story loses context the story's pathos—the ability to stir emotions—weakens and the logic behind an action becomes unclear.

Before Excerpt from "Burgundy Wayfarer"

This excerpt shows how losing context disrupts logic:

> "It's not yet raining." She points in the distance.
> "Everyone is running there." She yanks me up and runs into the water.

An editor unfamiliar to my story said she was confused about why it mattered to the story's characters whether it rained or not. She questioned what "there" refers to in Ate's dialogue.

After

Thus, I added context clues that add reason to the character's actions.

> "It's not yet raining. There's still time." She points in the distance. "Everyone is running to that crowd. Dad might be there." She yanks me up and runs into the water.

Context

Before Excerpt from "Burgundy Wayfarer"

The following shows how losing context weakens pathos:

> The corpses stack as their bodies bend in strange positions. A lifeguard pushes the chest of a young kid. My stomach tightens.

This excerpt didn't necessarily confuse the reader; rather it weakened the story's emotional appeal. In the feedback on my first draft, Gihad commented that she liked the detail about the kid wearing a Disney Princess outfit because this felt relatable and strengthened the scene.

After

> The corpses stack with their bodies bent in strange positions. A lifeguard resuscitates a girl wearing her Disney Princess swimsuit. My stomach tightens.

First Impressions

Candice Dela Cruz

The gel pen spins. "I wonder who's gonna read first?" I say, looking at Katherine, Marlie, and Gihad's faces staring at the twirling pen. The pen slows, wobbles, and then stops. It points at me. I groan and they sigh from relief.

"Please don't judge me. Writing two thousand words is tough," I say, gathering the sheets of paper.

"Don't worry. That's why we have a whole semester to fix everything," Marlie says grabbing paper from her bag. "So, we're starting with strengths, weaknesses, and opportunities, right?"

Gihad nods as she slides her pencil tip across the notebook to make a chart. "Yeah, just start whenever you're ready."

My voice shakes as I read the first sentence, "I dip my toes into the grey sand and glare at the grey skies and watch the grey waves leap on the shore." As I read my story's alliterations, parallelisms, and awful clichés, I hear furious scribbling.

The story ends and clapping ensues. Marlie looks at Gihad and Katherine, Katherine scribbles comments on her paper, and Gihad scans her notes. Silence creeps in.

"It's good," Gihad comments. "The story made me shiver, especially the part when you tiptoed and saw the pale, wrinkled toes."

"Oh, yeah! I like that part too. The story has good details," Katherine comments, "but I feel like you should be more consistent with your age. Sometimes I thought you were a kid, other times I thought you were older."

"I was actually eleven or twelve years old."

"I see. Then, you should focus on that," Marlie answers.

"I agree," Gihad adds. "I think you should also increase the pace a bit at the beginning. It has good sentences, but you should emphasize the ending."

"Maybe I can recycle those sentences," I smile and scribble down their comments.

Chapter Two

loss *n.* a state of consciousness when emotions become hectic and thoughts disjointed, when feelings clash and words jumble, and when nonsense makes sense and reason is baffling. **loss of control** act without restraint.

Beksa Lala

Katherine Kurowski

Kneeling before a pile of clothing, I contemplate the green, ankle-length summer dress between my hands and scrunch my nose. The bedroom door's groan rivets my attention. Roko, Ciocia's Irish terrier, weaves between linen pants. I turn back and place the folded dress atop the clothes pile beside me.

"Why are you leaving that dress in Germany," Ciocia—aunt in Polish—asks.

My cheeks flush. "Because I don't want to take it."

"Kasia, Mama bought it for you. Take it."

My chest tightens. "But I don't *want* to take it, Ciocia."

"Kasia, why did Mama buy it for you if you don't want to take it?"

I panic. "I didn't ask her to buy it for me!"

I scramble off the floor, burst from the room, stumble over Roko, and run into the bathroom. I turn the lock—thrice before it clicks. I slam the toilet lid down and slump my trembling body atop it, rubbing my wet eyes.

"What's happening to me?"

Pain—I pinch the back of my hand—*might distract me!* A choke escapes my lips. *I need a distraction!*

The white- and blue-tiled room wavers as I count six bottles of hair-related products and one loofah by the bathtub; six toothbrushes, two hairbrushes, and one comb by the sink; one hairdryer, five towels, three washcloths, and one pair of scissors by the wall. Curses and hiccups punctuate the lemon-scented air. *I can't breathe!*

I climb onto the toilet lid and grip the edge of the tiled windowsill. I turn the window's handle downwards and shove. The summer morning's rain-scented air floods my face. The windswept raindrops sprinkle across my brow and stream down to mingle with my tears. I descend from the toilet and lumber to the ceramic sink. I pat cold-wetted cotton pads against my inflamed skin.

"I should call Mom and Dad and tell them about my vacation. Maybe that would make me feel better," I tell my mirror's reflection.

Emerging from the bathroom, I find the phone on the hallway's shelf and notice the bedroom is empty. Nudging the bedroom door shut with my foot, I dial the long-distance number home.

I am calm and composed, I am calm and composed, I am calm—
"Hello?"

"Hi Da—" *and not fucking composed!* I bury my face into a pillow to muffle the weeping.

"Uh … we went to Centennial Park yesterday," Dad distracts. I sob.

"Mark barbequed kebabs, Mary helped Mama wash the dishes, John set the—"

I choke.

"Tita Ida's birthday is—"

I wheeze.

"Kasia! What's wrong," Dad demands. "Are you hurt? Did someone hurt you?"

I hyperventilate in response. *I wish someone had hurt me, then I would have a reason to cry, but I don't have a reason! I don't know why I am crying!* I cram the feather-stuffed pillow into my mouth and bite. *I am going to die!*

The mattress dips. The phone is taken from my shaky, weak grip. Incoherent yelling erupts from the phone's speaker and indignation replies. The dial tone beeps. I hiccup.

"Tata is upset with me, Kasia," Ciocia chides. "He thinks I did something to upset you."

I moan.

"Beksa lala." Crybaby.

I run to the bathroom. Five tries before the lock clicks.

———

"Distraction number two thousand and one: walk the dog," I sniffle.

My Converse's heels drag on the pavement and slosh through the puddles. Roko, tugging on the leash circling my snot-covered black cuffs, leads us from Ciocia's apartment down Strassen street—

What's wrong with me? Why am I such a crybaby?

Past Barbroicher Road—

And over a dress? It doesn't make sense.

And down Asselborner Lane—

My face hurts, my eczema. I rubbed it too hard.

Past some house-lined street—
I'm so ugly, an ugly crybaby.
And down another—
Ugly, ugly, ugly, ugly!
A left turn past a playground—
Why can't I calm down? What is up with these tears? Stop crying!
Across a meadow—
Oh, for goodness' sake, count the dandelions! One dandelion, two, three, four—

"Roko, no! Stop sniffing that." I tug him away from the litter amidst the dewy grass and we turn right towards a hill— *just breathe. Breathe*—and plod up the hill—*stop crying, stop crying, stop cry—*

"Wait, where are we?"

Red-clay-shingled and white-stucco-walled houses surround us. A shiver slithers up my spine.

"Uh . . . " I swivel to face Roko, "I thought this was your regular route with Ciocia! Now where have you led us to?"

Roko lifts his hind leg under the dripping bough of a maple.

"Humph." I scan the two rows of houses, the slick two-lane street, the two-car garages, and then my two sodden sneakers. I bring my cuff to my sniffling nose. *Don't panic.* The leash tightens around my wrist. Roko pulls me up the hill. Down the hill a rubber-booted woman manoeuvres around puddles with a pomeranian. Roko yips.

"Sorry."

The pair strolls away, snubbing us.

"Oh, I spoke in English." I realize.

"*Danke schoen?* No, that's *thank you.*"

"*Hund?*" No, that's *dog.*"

"*Gracias?* No, that's *Spanish*!"

Why do I suck at everything? I can't even go for a walk without getting lost.

"Where are we?" I lament.

At the hill's crest, I see only the unfamiliar: a house I don't recognize, another house I don't recognize, and a third house I don't recognize.

God hel—Wait! A spire!

"Roko! The church's spire! I know how to get back to Ciocia's from there!"

Keeping the spire in sight, we stride past the three houses and three more blocks of unfamiliar rows of houses. Turning the corner—*I know where we are!*—we pass Edeka-Markt where Ciocia buys groceries and the high school where my cousins attend.

My heartbeat slows and my steps falter. In front of St. Antonius Abbas church, I pause and smile up at the crucifix-tipped spire. I look down at Roko sniffing the cedar's trunk. "And you were never scared. Of course."

We return to Ciocia's apartment down Ball Street.

Economy

Details add to the story the way actions may not. Rather than have a character state the presence of an object or person, providing a sensory detail of the environment, such as a sound, a taste, or a tactile sensation, can express a characteristic that the reader can imagine and maybe empathize with.

Certain details, like proper nouns, provide inherent information and reduce the word count. For example, a "medium-sized dog" is less specific than an "Irish terrier." The author does not need to describe its type of fur or its facial structure and how this "medium-sized dog" contrasts with other dogs because "Irish terrier" contains that information in two words.

Details do not always support the story and the unnecessary ones may drag its pace. This is when "cutting" takes place. Cut all extraneous details. Cut all characters that don't add value to the plot. Cut all events that don't support the main story. Details are memorable, but too much can cloud the reader's psychic space and prevent the reader from seeing the important picture. As an editor, point out parts of the story that may be cut out. Keep the story tight.

Before Excerpt from "Beksa Lala"

In an early draft, my introduction was lengthy and confusing. I included a character, my cousin Klara, who did not support my story, and unnecessary information about my vacation plans.

> I pack for my trip to Głogów, a town in Poland to spend the rest of my summer vacation, when my aunt Theresa comes into the room I share with my cousin Klara. A green summer dress lies atop a mount of clothes assigned to remain in Germany until I return back from Poland for when I leave Europe for home from the airport in Dusseldorf.

After

In the final draft, I removed the mention of my cousin and my confusing itinerary. I introduced the important characters sooner: Roko weaving between Ciocia's linen pants. I illustrated, rather than stated, the action of assigning the dress to a pile.

> Kneeling before a pile of clothing, I contemplate the green, ankle-length summer dress between my hands and scrunch my nose. The bedroom door's groan rivets my attention. Roko, Ciocia's Irish terrier, weaves between linen pants. I turn back and place the folded dress atop the clothes pile beside me.

I cut my word count from sixty-four to fifty and also tightened the introduction by focusing on the big picture and omitting details that complicated the storyline.

STYLISTIC EDITING

Maria Rivera

"It's not personal."

I've never edited so many drafts in my entire life.
They want me to use a stronger verb?
Does this scene flow?
Constructive Criticism. Constructive. Criticism.
I reread this sentence four times now.
Wait! I have to make sure this sentence sounds right. I need to read it aloud.
Don't tell me it's 2 a.m. already.
Hey, can you listen to this and let me know what you think?
What do you mean draft G?

"Remember these changes are always optional."

What kind of picture do you get when you hear the word "infest?"
Should I choose "drag" or "weigh?"

The Hard Copy

I only need to cut six more words.
Make sure it flows.
Show, not tell.
There are too many comments.
Wait, I need to see if the symbols match.
I liked that word though.
I forgot to finish a sentence, my bad.

Chapter Three

loss *n*. loss is difficult to grasp. Loss is equivocal. You struggle to feel and so you force, you perform, you fake your grief. **loss is nothing**.

Missed Call

Gihad Nasr

"Mom! Dad's phone is ringing."

Mom sits on the bed with Nancy's mom chatting and laughing and flailing her hands in the air.

Riiiiiing! Riiiiiing!

I push myself off the Barbie-littered floor, scamper around Lena and Nancy to the bedside table, and snatch Dad's cell phone.

"Mom! Aunt Lina's calling!"

She tilts her head and furrows her brows. Creases form on her forehead, wrinkles paint the corners of her eyes, and freckles peer through the melted foundation on her face.

"We have guests over now." Mom's eyelids fall. "Your dad's gonna have to call her back."

The phone keeps ringing as I drop it on the bed and sprint to my Barbies without looking back. For the rest of the night, I babble and laugh and crack jokes with Nancy and Lena. And Dad? Dad doesn't call Aunt Lina back.

———

The clock reads 8:23 a.m. I fling the sheets into the air, hop off the bed, gather my hair into a ponytail, pull my socks on, scurry to the closet, scramble through the folded pile of clothing, and tug at the sleeves of my oversized, red Roots sweater.

"What?! Is she okay," Mom roars from the living room. "Last night?!"

Lena and Abood, my younger siblings, race into my bedroom.

"It has to do with Aunt Lina!"

"I heard she was in a car accident!"

"She died."

Mom's sniffles fill the house.

The sweater slips through my hands. Died? I tiptoe out of my bedroom and follow the flashing, blue lights illuminating the end of the narrow, dim hallway. Abood and Lena trail behind.

A clear plastic bag of pita bread lies open on the coffee table. A pan of untouched scrambled eggs and an electric kettle rest on either side of the bread. Mom and Dad huddle together on the black, leather sofa against the wall. The television lights reflect off their faces. Tears roll down Mom's freckled cheeks. Skin peels off her pale lips, eye bags jut underneath her lids, and a glossy film covers the whites of her eyes.

"I'm sure she died," Abood whispers.

"Don't say that," I mouth back. I turn back to Mom and Dad. "Did she…die," I probe.

Mom nods. "Go get ready for school. You're going," she croaks.

Dad screws his eyes shut, purses his lips, and breathes through his flared nostrils. He digs his fingernails into his palm and speaks, "I was the last person she called."

Mom and Dad hold a reception at our house. Friends gather, shed tears, drink coffee, nibble on dates, recite prayers, and drink more coffee.

I cross my legs, place my hands in my lap, and wait for the details of the accident.

"Her two brothers sided with her husband during the argument," Mom begins. "She escaped out of the apartment . . ."

A weight settles on my chest.

". . . and raced down the corridor."

I sink my teeth into the inside of my cheeks.

"Then she disappeared," Mom dabs the corners of her eyes with a tissue, "behind the elevator doors before anyone could chase after her." Mom wraps her fingers around the coffee mug. "They thought she'd come around." She lifts the mug to her lips. "But she didn't." She takes a sip. "She called my husband last night, right before the accident. Wanted to speak to him. Maybe to vent to him." Mom lets out a heavy sigh. "No one answered."

With trembling hands, Mom reaches for her cell phone and turns it towards her friends. A high-pitched wail startles me. I squint at the photograph.

The driver's door of a silver Jeep dangles by its hinges. Metal debris scatters the pavement. The car's hood splits through the windshield, shards of crimson-tainted glass glint in the darkness, and a tire rests against the curb. In the background, a white sheet cloaks a figure lying on the pavement.

"She was speeding on a roundabout."

I push my chair back, slip out of the dining room, and sneak into my bedroom. The image of my aunt, blinking away tears and frantically dialling Dad's number while racing down the freeway in her silver Jeep, flashes through my mind.

"Are you crying?" Lena towers over me with a date in her right hand and a glass of orange juice in her left.

"I'm not crying." I'm not. I ignore Lena's smirk and go over the details in my head.

Aunt Lina, who left a four-year-old daughter behind, had sent a text to Mom earlier that week. My aunt Lina, who left two sons behind, had texted about death. My aunt Lina, who Lena is named after, took the elevator down to her death.

"Do you think it was... on purpose," I ask Lena.

"You mean suicide?"

I nod. "What if the accident wasn't an accident?"

"It wasn't," Lena responds.

Parallelism

Writers strive to create easy-to-read, straightforward, and smooth pieces of writing. The technique of parallelism showcases this balance in writing best. Read the first sentence. Do you notice the clarity? Do you notice the structure? Do you notice the efficiency?

Parallelism is the repetition of grammatical structure, such as in the first sentence of this chapter. The first sentence contains three adjectival phrases. The first paragraph's fourth, fifth, and sixth sentences exemplify perfect parallelism in which three distinct sentences contain similar structure. They all begin with, "Do you notice..."

Parallelism

Before Excerpt from "Missed Call"

Now take an excerpt from my story's first draft:

> Lines form on her forehead and under her eyes. Her freckles peer through her melted foundation.

Do you notice how I express my ideas in two distinct sentences that do not follow a similar structure? The excerpt's first sentence begins with a noun, and the second sentence with a pronoun. To improve this, I can rephrase the second sentence to mirror the first: "Lines form on her forehead. Wrinkles paint the corners of her eyes. Freckles peer through her melted foundation." Now each sentence begins with a noun and performs an action.

After

Although this example is one way of employing perfect parallelism, my final draft contains parallelism within the sentence:

> Creases form on her forehead, wrinkles paint the corners of her eyes, and freckles peer through the melted foundation caked on her face.

All three clauses begin with a noun and are written in the active voice. To employ parallelism, structure your clauses or sentences similarly to produce a balanced, easy-to-read, and creative piece.

COPYEDITING

Gihad Nasr

Original

Who said Copyediting was a peace of cake? It's not. "Just follow the guidelines in the Chicago manual of style and mark the paper," they say. Copyediting is one of the last stages before publication. "So you have to pay extra attention to detail." Consistency. Consistency. Consistency. Grammer. Spelling. Select one style: american spelling or Canadian spelling. Color or colour? Gray or grey?

Don't forget the principles of punctuation. Use spaced suspension points (commonly refered to as an ellipsis) ... to suggest falering speech. But use an em dash—with no space before or after—to indicate sudden interuptions in thought or dialogue. They can also set off an explanatory element in place of comma. Look for formatting errors: indentation, spacing, font style, and the treatment of numbers. Whoops! I forgot to indent this paragraph. How many times do I have to reread this? Draft 6 already? Wait! Spell out numbers below 101. Italicize foreign words when you introduce them on first occurence.

Look for errors in titles, subtitles, and footnotes. Reread the story from the beginning to the end. And finally, read it from the end to the beginning.

Edited

Who said copyediting was a piece of cake? It's not. "Just follow the guidelines in *The Chicago Manual of Style* and mark the paper," they say. Copyediting is one of the last stages before publication. "So you have to pay extra attention to detail." Consistency. Consistency. Consistency. Grammar. Spelling. Select one style: American spelling or Canadian spelling. Color or colour? Gray or grey?

Don't forget the principles of punctuation. Use spaced suspension points (commonly referred to as an ellipsis) . . . to suggest faltering speech. But use an em dash—with no space before or after—to indicate sudden interuptions in thought or dialogue. They can also set off an explanatory element in place of commas.

Look for formatting errors: indentation, spacing, font style, and the treatment of numbers. Whoops! I forgot to indent this paragraph. How many times do I have to reread this? Draft six already? Wait! Spell out numbers below 101. Italicize foreign words when you introduce them on first occurence.

Look for errors in titles, subtitles, and footnotes. Reread the story from the beginning to the end. And finally, read it from the end to the beginning.

Chapter Four

loss *n.* electricity radiates from the core, runs through the bones, and escapes through the extremities leaving one empty. **loss of sensation. loss of identity.**

Only a Shell

Maria Rivera

Copper pans, dishes, and silverware clatter in the kitchen. The exhaust fan's buzz vibrates throughout the house. A knife chops a steady beat. Reaching the second floor, the scent of garlic and onion invade my nose and sting my eyes. Sunlight pours through the window by the staircase, casting intricate shadows beyond the frosted glass.

I rub my eyes and squint at the brightness. Donning an old pair of blue shorts from Ate—older sister in Filipino—and a loose t-shirt, I peek between the second-floor's railings that overlook the main hallway.

"Mommy . . . Mo . . . I need . . . I need to go to the washroom. I have to pee," Ate orders in a lagging, distorted voice.

I purse my lips as my hand grips the wooden rail.

"*Tama na!* I'm doing something in the kitchen," Mom commands. The freezer rolls open and shut. A splash follows. "You just went an hour ago and you need to go again? You always say this. Normal people don't pee every fifteen minutes. This isn't normal."

"But I . . . have to go really bad and the sound of the water isn't helping."

"It's almost nine o'clock. Just wait until the PSW comes. Until then, hold it in. I'm trying to make lunch," Mom begs.

"Okay," Ate mumbles from her thousand-dollar electronic hospital bed. Maxxi, my eight-year-old miniature schnauzer, looks up at me from the foot of the staircase. I raise my brows.

"Watchu lookin' at," I mouth.

She tilts her head.

I inch away from the railings and tiptoe towards my bedroom. My fingers slip through the crack of the door, wrap around its edge, and push it open without making a sound.

Cool air rushes out from the floor vent. Goosebumps sweep along my exposed skin. My knees give in and I slide down to the hardwood floor. Across from me hangs my sky-blue rosary that Mom gave me. During Ate's comatose, my family resorted to hour-long rosary sessions; reciting decades of Hail Marys became routine. I massage my throbbing temples and exhale.

> Our Father, who art in heaven . . . Hail Mary, full
> of grace . . . Lord, please keep my family, Maxxi, my
> friends, and me strong, healthy, and safe. I hope Ate re-
> covers quickly. Help me find a good job. Please? Thank
> You for getting us through every day.

I reach for my forehead.

> In the name of the Father, the Son, and the Holy
> Spirit, Amen.

I rise to my feet, eyeing my desk. Photographs of family vacations, stationery, and notebooks bury my study space. I wedge the notebooks in-between Ate's old Finding Nemo bookends and stack the stationery on the side. I slip the photographs from our last vacation into an album titled Boracay 2011. Vivid memories rush into my mind.

———

We return from the Philippines at summer's end. I retreat to my bedroom from the Saturday rowdiness: Mom and Dad shuffling, Rollo clicking away at his laptop, Maxxi barking, and Ate groaning. Conversation floats to the second floor.

"Diana, *anak*, what's wrong," Dad booms.

"I'm dizzy. My chest feels heavy." Footsteps drag towards the family room. "I need my puffer." The leather sofa releases a hiss of air as somebody thuds onto it.

"*Ay*, you're always so dramatic. Just rest, drink water, and wait. If it doesn't improve, we'll go to the hospital," Dad replies.

A click of static wakens the TV, " . . . sunny day today."

"Diana! What's wrong with you," he panics.

I shoot up from my bed and speed towards the commotion.

"Diana!"

"Ate!"

Screams infest the room. My heart plunges.

"*Anak*, wake up! *Anak*," Mom screams, shaking Diana. Ate convulses, her limbs stiffen, her eyes roll back, and her body dips into the couch. Chunky, yellow bile pours out from her mouth onto the floor, revealing the lunch we had. Mom trembles, holding her up. She sticks her fist into Ate's mouth to prevent her from biting her tongue. I stand frozen in the hallway. Maxxi's barking cuts through the air. The room spins around the sight of my sister. My younger brother, Rollo, restrains Maxxi away from Ate. My stomach tightens.

"I have an emergency. We live on Bentley," Dad notifies, failing to hide the wobble in his voice. "It's been about five minutes. Thank you."

I attempt to inch closer, but my feet remain stiff. Mom yelps as teeth dig into her skin. I cave and dart to Ate's side.

"Ate! Wake up! Listen to my voice!" I squeeze and pinch Ate's limbs. I hold her steady, entwining our fingers. Her fingers untangle from mine. My wide eyes flicker from Mom's bleeding fist to Rollo hugging Maxxi to the bile beside my foot to Dad clearing obstructions. I jolt back at the sound of footsteps entering the house.

"Please clear the area," a paramedic instructs. Rollo carries Maxxi away. I step back as they rush to Ate. One paramedic tends to Mom's hand. Strapping my sister onto a stretcher, they haul her limp body outside.

"We'll call you later. Please help clean up the mess here," Dad instructs. "We'll be back soon." My parents follow the response team outdoors.

Eyeing the bile on the floor, I grab some paper towels and begin to clean.

The six-year-old vacation album lays on the desk, warm under the sunlight. I hear the water running and the caretaker humming, coming from Ate's bathroom downstairs. I stand in front of the clock on my bookshelf, duster in hand. My limbs grow numb, my throat swells, and a familiar weight resurfaces. My vision fixates on a photograph of the whole family in front of a giant sandcastle. My eyelids droop, heavy on my face. I think about Ate before the incident—my roommate, my role model, and my best friend. I swallow the lump in my throat. Sitting on top of the shelf is the puka shell bracelet—a string laced with hollow beige- and peach-coloured shells—which Ate bought in Boracay. I replace the duster in my hand with the bracelet and rub the shells between my fingers. I rarely wear it; Ate wanted to wear it first.

Three months after the incident, Ate woke up from her coma —with stitches scars on her scalp and tubes in her stomach— leaving behind any trace of herself.

Active Voice

In most literature, the active voice is a writer's best friend. The active voice is clarity and economy. It does not leave the reader confused. A sentence written in the active voice contains an active subject—that is, the subject performing the verb. The active voice paints vivid pictures and enriches the reader's psychic space.

In contrast, the passive voice may be vague, confusing, and awkward to read. This doesn't mean that writers should rule out the use of passive voice. Writers can use the passive voice when the actor is irrelevant or unknown. In stylistic and structural editing, the editor must detect whether it's appropriate to use the passive voice. However, try to use active voice at every opportunity to breathe life into your work.

Before Excerpt from "Only a Shell"

There were several instances when I wrote in the passive voice instead of the active. Here are two excerpts from my early draft of "Only a Shell."

> The iPhone was cautiously laid to rest on the drawing table that was handed down to me by my family friends.

> During the months my sister was in a coma, apart from reaching out to friends for help, my family resorted to prayer.

After

After going through several iterations, I omitted the first sentence because of its wordiness and irrelevance. I improved the second sentence in the final draft.

> During Ate's coma, my family resorted to hour-long rosary sessions; reciting decades of Hail Marys became routine.

Rewriting the first example in the active voice solved its passiveness and wordiness. While I added words to the second example, I tightened the details and incorporated surrounding sentences to make one active sentence.

Compiling the Manuscript

Candice Dela Cruz

"Don't worry. That's why we have a whole semester to fix everything."
Hearing this made me happy. From the Google Docs we made to the Facebook group we formed to the weekly meetings we agreed on, I felt reassured that we could rely on each other.

Marlie kept track of our meeting's agenda and our to-do lists, and updated the Facebook group with our objectives. I think she's brave to write her story about her family's challenges during her older sister's coma. In the first meeting, we had trouble understanding her story's timeline because the story went back and forth between the present and the past. However, our team reassured her that we would polish her story to its best form.

Gihad gave great advice during our meetings. She started our team's mantra: be harsh and bring out the harsh edits. She shared her experience about her aunt's accident with vivid, almost poetic, details. Gihad's attitude towards improving our team's writing is valued and appreciated. She pushed us to showcase our work's best qualities. In her story, she expressed her challenge over feeling indifferent at the news of her aunt's death. We encouraged her to be genuine. She didn't need to force sorrow if she didn't feel it.

Katherine joined our group last. Most of the groups in class struggled to find a fourth member, but Gihad, Marlie, and I hustled to invite Katherine to our team. Katherine is observant. During our meetings, when we talk about topics unrelated to our agenda, she redirects our discussions and reminds us of our focus. Katherine's story is about her vacation in Germany. Our team liked her story, but we agreed that she needed a focus. We suggested she focus her theme of loss on losing self-control—her panic attack—or on losing her way back to Ciocia's apartment.

Each member of our team brought value to our manuscript. We may have disagreed at times—like on the portfolio's theme, the meeting's location, or the creative entries—but our shared goal pushed us to support each other's work. It's amazing how every story came to be our own. It's neither Marlie's story nor Gihad's story nor Katherine's story nor Candice's story: it's the team's story.

About the Authors

CANDICE DELA CRUZ is a third-year digital enterprise management (DEM) and professional writing and communication student. Candice watches documentaries and anime, designs graphic projects and websites, and plants gardenias and roses in the summer. She is the president of the DEM Society, the organizer of the Young Entrepreneurs Conference, and a committee member of the UTM Film Fest.

KATHERINE KUROWSKI majors in biology for health sciences and minors in biomedical communications. She loves wildflowers—gets upset if you call them weeds—and photographing them. Katherine enjoys reading gothic novels and scrapbooking.

GIHAD NASR studies criminology and professional writing and communication at the University of Toronto. Gihad watches crime documentaries and reads up on criminal justice issues. Attending court during her spare time inspires her to write about her experiences.

MARIA RIVERA specializes in digital enterprise management and minors in professional writing and communication at the University of Toronto's Mississauga campus. Maria goes by Marlie to close friends and family. She sometimes roams around the GTA capturing urban spaces with her camera, draws with a hot mug of milk tea nearby, and dabbles in personal graphic and web design projects.

www.ingramcontent.com/pod-product-compliance
Lightning Source LLC
Chambersburg PA
CBHW071231160426
43196CB00012B/2477